Table of Contents

Chapter 1: Understanding Wishpond Lead Generation 5

    1.1 What is Wishpond? 5

    1.2 The Importance of Lead Generation 6

    1.3 How Wishpond Can Help Your Business 7

    1.4 Key Features of Wishpond for Lead Generation 9

    1.5 Common Challenges in Lead Generation 10

    1.6 Setting Goals for Lead Generation with Wishpond 12

Chapter 2: Getting Started with Wishpond 15

    2.1 Signing Up for Wishpond 15

    2.2 Navigating the Wishpond Dashboard 16

    2.3 Understanding Wishpond Pricing Plans 16

    2.4 Integrating Wishpond with Your Website 17

    2.5 Customizing Wishpond Campaigns 18

    2.6 Best Practices for Setting Up Your Wishpond Account 19

Chapter 3: Creating Effective Landing Pages 22

    3.1 The Importance of Landing Pages in Lead Generation 22

    3.2 Designing High-Converting Landing Pages with Wishpond 24

    3.3 Optimizing Landing Page Content for Conversions 25

3.4 A/B Testing Your Landing Pages with Wishpond 26

3.5 Integrating Landing Pages with Email Marketing 27

3.6 Tracking Landing Page Performance Metrics.............. 28

Chapter 4: Mastering Email Marketing with Wishpond 31

4.1 Building Your Email List with Wishpond 31

4.2 Designing Engaging Email Campaigns......................... 32

4.3 Personalizing Email Content with Wishpond.............. 33

4.4 Automating Email Workflows with Wishpond............ 34

4.5 Analyzing Email Campaign Performance 36

4.6 Tips for Email Marketing Success with Wishpond 37

Chapter 5: Harnessing Social Media for Lead Generation 40

5.1 Leveraging Social Media Platforms with Wishpond ... 40

5.2 Creating Contests and Promotions on Social Media... 41

5.3 Integrating Social Media with Your Wishpond Campaigns.. 42

5.4 Engaging with Your Social Media Audience................ 43

5.5 Analyzing Social Media Metrics with Wishpond......... 44

5.6 Case Studies: Successful Social Media Lead Generation Strategies 45

Chapter 6: Using Wishpond for Marketing Automation....... 48

6.1 Understanding Marketing Automation with Wishpond 48

6.2 Creating Automated Workflows for Lead Nurturing .. 50

6.3 Segmenting Your Audience with Wishpond 51

6.4 Personalizing Customer Journeys with Automation ... 53

6.5 Integrating Wishpond with CRM Systems 55

6.6 Monitoring and Optimizing Marketing Automation Performance 56

Chapter 7: Optimizing Conversions with Wishpond 59

7.1 The Importance of Conversion Optimization 59

7.2 Using Wishpond's Conversion Tracking Tools 60

7.3 Implementing A/B Testing for Conversion Rate Optimization 61

7.4 Analyzing User Behavior with Wishpond 62

7.5 Improving Conversion Funnels with Wishpond Insights 64

7.6 Case Studies: Successful Conversion Optimization Strategies 65

Chapter 8: Scaling Your Lead Generation Efforts 68

8.1 Strategies for Scaling Lead Generation with Wishpond 68

8.2 Expanding Your Reach with Wishpond's Growth Tools 70

8.3 Collaborating with Partners for Joint Lead Generation Campaigns 71

8.4 Leveraging Paid Advertising with Wishpond 73

8.5 Monitoring and Adjusting Your Scaling Strategies 74

    8.6 Future Trends in Lead Generation and Wishpond's Role 76

Chapter 9: Troubleshooting Common Issues with Wishpond 79

    9.1 Identifying and Resolving Technical Issues 79

    9.2 Addressing Low Conversion Rates 82

    9.3 Dealing with Deliverability Problems in Email Marketing.. 84

    9.4 Overcoming Integration Challenges........................... 86

    9.5 Handling Customer Support and Feedback 88

    9.6 Tips for Preventing Future Issues................................ 90

Chapter 10: Measuring Success and ROI with Wishpond 93

    10.1 Defining Key Performance Indicators (KPIs) for Lead Generation 93

    10.2 Tracking and Analyzing Metrics with Wishpond Analytics 95

    10.3 Calculating Return on Investment (ROI) for Wishpond Campaigns... 96

    10.4 Reporting on Lead Generation Success to Stakeholders 98

    10.5 Iterating and Improving Your Lead Generation Strategies 99

    10.6 Celebrating Successes and Setting New Goals........ 101

Conclusion.. 103

Chapter 1: Understanding Wishpond Lead Generation

Lead generation is a fundamental aspect of any business's growth strategy. In today's digital age, where competition is fierce and consumer behavior is constantly evolving, effective lead generation can make or break a company's success. Wishpond, a comprehensive marketing platform, offers businesses a suite of tools to streamline and optimize their lead generation efforts. To grasp the significance and potential of Wishpond, it's essential to delve into its functionality, benefits, and how it addresses common challenges in lead generation.

1.1 What is Wishpond?

Wishpond is a cloud-based marketing software designed to help businesses generate leads, nurture relationships with prospects, and drive conversions. Founded in 2009, Wishpond has evolved into a versatile platform offering a range of marketing solutions, including email marketing, landing pages, social promotions, and marketing automation. At its core, Wishpond aims to empower businesses of all sizes to attract, engage, and retain customers through targeted campaigns and personalized interactions.

Wishpond's user-friendly interface and customizable templates make it accessible to marketers with varying levels of expertise. Whether you're a small startup looking to establish an online presence or a seasoned enterprise seeking to optimize your marketing funnel, Wishpond provides the tools and analytics needed to achieve your goals. From lead capture forms to automated email workflows, Wishpond offers a comprehensive toolkit to support every stage of the customer journey.

1.2 The Importance of Lead Generation

Lead generation serves as the lifeblood of any business, driving growth and revenue by identifying and capturing potential customers. In a competitive marketplace saturated with endless choices, businesses must actively engage with prospects and provide value to stand out from the crowd. Effective lead generation enables companies to expand their reach, build brand awareness, and cultivate relationships with qualified leads.

Without a consistent influx of leads, businesses risk stagnation and eventual decline. Lead generation lays the foundation for sustainable growth by continuously replenishing the sales pipeline with fresh opportunities. By leveraging innovative strategies and technologies like Wishpond, businesses can enhance their lead generation efforts and stay ahead of the curve in today's dynamic landscape.

1.3 How Wishpond Can Help Your Business

Wishpond offers a comprehensive suite of tools and features designed to streamline and optimize lead generation efforts. By harnessing the power of Wishpond, businesses can effectively attract, engage, and convert prospects into loyal customers. Let's explore some ways in which Wishpond can benefit your business:

- **Streamlined Campaign Creation:** Wishpond's intuitive drag-and-drop editor allows users to create professional-looking landing pages, forms, and email campaigns without any coding skills required. This streamlines the campaign creation process and enables marketers to launch campaigns quickly and efficiently.

- **Lead Nurturing Automation:** Wishpond's marketing automation features enable businesses to automate repetitive tasks and deliver personalized experiences to leads at every stage of the buyer's journey. From automated email drip campaigns to behavior-based triggers, Wishpond empowers businesses to nurture leads effectively and move them closer to conversion.

- **Advanced Analytics:** Wishpond provides comprehensive analytics and reporting tools to track the performance of your marketing campaigns in real-time. By monitoring key metrics such as conversion rates, lead quality, and campaign ROI, businesses can make data-driven decisions and optimize their strategies for maximum impact.

- **Integration Capabilities:** Wishpond seamlessly integrates with popular CRM platforms, email marketing tools, and e-commerce platforms, allowing businesses to consolidate their marketing efforts and streamline data management. Whether you're using Salesforce, Mailchimp, or Shopify, Wishpond offers seamless integration to enhance your workflow.

1.4 Key Features of Wishpond for Lead Generation

Wishpond offers a wide range of features specifically designed to facilitate lead generation and conversion. Let's explore some of the key features that make Wishpond a powerful tool for businesses:

- **Customizable Landing Pages:** Wishpond's drag-and-drop landing page builder enables users to create visually stunning and conversion-optimized landing pages without any coding knowledge. With customizable templates and A/B testing capabilities, businesses can maximize their landing page performance and capture more leads.

- **Lead Capture Forms:** Wishpond provides customizable lead capture forms that can be easily embedded on your website, blog, or social media pages. From simple contact forms to multi-step quizzes, Wishpond offers a variety of form options to capture leads effectively and qualify them based on specific criteria.

- **Email Marketing Automation:** Wishpond's email marketing automation features enable businesses to send targeted and personalized emails to leads based on their behavior and preferences. From welcome emails to abandoned cart reminders, Wishpond automates the email workflow to nurture leads and drive conversions.

- **Social Promotions:** Wishpond allows businesses to run engaging social media contests, sweepstakes, and promotions to attract new followers and generate leads. With built-in sharing features and customizable entry forms, Wishpond makes it easy to harness the power of social media for lead generation.

- **Marketing Automation Workflows:** Wishpond's marketing automation workflows enable businesses to automate repetitive tasks and deliver personalized experiences to leads based on their actions and interests. From lead scoring to lead segmentation, Wishpond empowers businesses to tailor their marketing efforts to the unique needs of each prospect.

1.5 Common Challenges in Lead Generation

While lead generation is essential for business growth, it also poses several challenges that can hinder success. From attracting qualified leads to nurturing them through the sales funnel, businesses must navigate various obstacles to achieve their lead generation goals. Some common challenges in lead generation include:

- **Lead Quality:** Generating a high volume of leads is meaningless if they lack quality and relevance. Identifying and attracting qualified leads that are likely to convert into customers requires careful targeting and segmentation.

- **Lead Engagement:** Once leads are captured, engaging and nurturing them through personalized interactions can be challenging. From email fatigue to content overload, businesses must find creative ways to keep leads engaged and interested in their products or services.

- **Conversion Optimization:** Converting leads into customers requires more than just capturing their contact information. Businesses must deliver value, address pain points, and provide compelling reasons for leads to take action.

- **Data Management:** Managing and organizing lead data can quickly become overwhelming, especially as the volume of leads increases. Without proper data management processes in place, businesses may struggle to effectively track and analyze lead interactions.

- **Competition:** In today's competitive landscape, businesses must differentiate themselves and stand out from competitors vying for the same pool of leads. Finding unique selling points and delivering exceptional experiences can help businesses rise above the competition.

1.6 Setting Goals for Lead Generation with Wishpond

To maximize the effectiveness of Wishpond for lead generation, it's essential to set clear and achievable goals that align with your business objectives. Whether your goal is to increase brand awareness, drive website traffic, or boost sales, Wishpond offers a range of tools and features to support your objectives. Here are some tips for setting goals for lead generation with Wishpond:

1. **Define Your Objectives:** Start by defining specific, measurable, and time-bound objectives for your lead generation efforts. Whether you're aiming to increase lead capture rates, improve lead quality, or shorten the sales cycle, clearly defined goals will guide your strategy and measure success.

2. **Identify Your Target Audience:** Understand your target audience's demographics, interests, and pain points to tailor your lead generation efforts effectively. By creating buyer personas and segmenting your audience, you can deliver personalized experiences that resonate with potential leads.

3. **Choose the Right Tools and Features:** Explore Wishpond's suite of tools and features to identify those that best align with your goals and target audience. Whether you prioritize customizable landing pages, email marketing automation, or social promotions, choose the tools that will help you achieve your objectives most efficiently.

4. **Track Key Metrics:** Monitor key performance indicators (KPIs) such as lead conversion rates, engagement rates, and ROI to gauge the effectiveness of your lead generation efforts. By tracking and analyzing data regularly, you can identify areas for improvement and optimize your strategy for better results.

5. **Iterate and Improve:** Lead generation is an iterative process that requires continuous testing, refinement, and improvement. Experiment with different strategies,

messaging, and offers to see what resonates best with your audience, and don't be afraid to adapt and evolve your approach based on feedback and insights.

By setting clear goals, understanding your audience, leveraging the right tools, and continuously optimizing your strategy, you can harness the full potential of Wishpond for lead generation and drive sustainable growth for your business.

Chapter 2: Getting Started with Wishpond

Wishpond is a powerful platform that helps businesses of all sizes create, manage, and optimize their marketing campaigns effectively. Whether you're a small startup or a large corporation, Wishpond offers a range of features and tools to streamline your marketing efforts and drive better results. In this chapter, we'll dive into the basics of getting started with Wishpond, from signing up and navigating the dashboard to understanding pricing plans, integrating Wishpond with your website, customizing campaigns, and implementing best practices for setting up your account.

2.1 Signing Up for Wishpond

Signing up for Wishpond is a straightforward process that begins with visiting the Wishpond website and clicking on the "Sign Up" button. Once you've clicked on the button, you'll be prompted to provide some basic information such as your email address, company name, and desired password. After filling out the required fields, you'll need to agree to Wishpond's terms of service and privacy policy before completing the sign-up process.

Upon successful sign-up, you'll gain access to your Wishpond dashboard, where you can start exploring the various features and tools available to you.

Wishpond offers a free trial period for new users, allowing you to test out the platform and see if it meets your business needs before committing to a paid plan.

2.2 Navigating the Wishpond Dashboard

The Wishpond dashboard serves as the central hub for managing all aspects of your marketing campaigns. Upon logging in, you'll be greeted with an intuitive interface that allows you to easily navigate between different sections such as campaigns, leads, automation, analytics, and more.

One of the key features of the Wishpond dashboard is its customizable layout, which allows you to arrange and prioritize widgets according to your preferences. Whether you're monitoring the performance of your latest email campaign or creating a new landing page, you can quickly access the tools and insights you need with just a few clicks.

2.3 Understanding Wishpond Pricing Plans

Wishpond offers a range of pricing plans to accommodate businesses of all sizes and budgets. The pricing plans are tiered based on the number of leads you wish to capture and the features you require.

Here are some key points to consider when evaluating Wishpond pricing plans:

- **Features:** Each pricing tier offers a different set of features and tools. For example, higher-tier plans may include advanced automation capabilities, A/B testing, and CRM integration.

- **Leads Limit:** The number of leads you can capture each month varies depending on your selected plan. It's essential to choose a plan that aligns with your expected lead volume to avoid overage charges.

- **Billing Cycle:** Wishpond offers both monthly and annual billing options. Opting for an annual plan can often result in cost savings compared to paying month-to-month.

2.4 Integrating Wishpond with Your Website

Integrating Wishpond with your website is essential for seamlessly capturing leads and driving conversions. Wishpond provides various integration options, depending on your website platform and requirements.

Here are some common integration methods:

- **Embedding Forms:** Wishpond allows you to embed lead capture forms directly onto your website pages. Simply copy and paste the provided HTML code into your website's code editor to display the form seamlessly.

- **WordPress Plugin:** If you're using WordPress as your website platform, Wishpond offers a dedicated plugin for easy integration. Install the plugin, connect your Wishpond account, and start creating and embedding campaigns directly from your WordPress dashboard.

- **API Integration:** For more advanced users, Wishpond offers API integration, allowing you to connect your website's backend systems directly with Wishpond's platform. This enables seamless data synchronization and automation between your website and Wishpond.

2.5 Customizing Wishpond Campaigns

Customizing Wishpond campaigns is crucial for ensuring they resonate with your target audience and align with your brand identity. Wishpond offers a range of customization options for various campaign types, including landing pages, pop-ups, contests, and email campaigns.

Here are some customization options available within Wishpond:

- **Templates:** Wishpond provides a library of professionally designed templates for different campaign types. Choose a template that matches your brand aesthetics and customize it with your own images, colors, and messaging.

- **Drag-and-Drop Editor:** Wishpond's intuitive drag-and-drop editor allows you to customize every aspect of your campaigns without any coding knowledge. Easily rearrange elements, add custom fields to forms, and tweak design elements to create a unique look and feel.

- **Personalization:** Tailor your campaigns to specific audience segments using Wishpond's personalization features. Show different content or offers based on factors such as location, past behavior, or demographic information to maximize relevance and engagement.

2.6 Best Practices for Setting Up Your Wishpond Account

Setting up your Wishpond account effectively is essential for maximizing your marketing ROI and driving sustainable growth. Here are some best practices to consider when setting up your Wishpond account:

- **Define Your Goals:** Before diving into campaign creation, clearly define your marketing objectives and goals. Whether it's increasing leads, driving sales, or building brand awareness, having a clear goal in mind will guide your campaign strategy.

- **Segment Your Audience:** Take advantage of Wishpond's audience segmentation capabilities to target specific customer segments with tailored messaging and offers. By segmenting your audience based on factors such as demographics, interests, or purchase history, you can deliver more relevant and personalized experiences.

- **Test and Iterate:** Continuously test different elements of your campaigns, such as subject lines, images, and calls-to-action, to optimize performance over time. Use Wishpond's A/B testing feature to compare variations and identify what resonates best with your audience.

- **Monitor and Analyze:** Regularly monitor campaign performance metrics such as conversion rates, click-through rates, and lead quality to track progress towards your goals. Use Wishpond's analytics dashboard to gain insights into which campaigns are performing well and where there's room for improvement.

By following these best practices, you can unlock the full potential of Wishpond and drive meaningful results for your business.

Chapter 3: Creating Effective Landing Pages

In the world of digital marketing, landing pages are the unsung heroes, quietly playing a pivotal role in lead generation strategies. These seemingly simple web pages hold immense power, acting as the first point of contact between a potential customer and a business. Yet, their importance often goes underestimated, overshadowed by flashy ad campaigns and social media strategies. However, savvy marketers understand that the effectiveness of landing pages can make or break a campaign. Let's delve into the intricacies of creating landing pages that not only capture attention but also convert visitors into valuable leads.

3.1 The Importance of Landing Pages in Lead Generation

Landing pages serve as the gateway to conversions in the online realm. Unlike a homepage or a generic web page, a landing page is meticulously crafted to guide visitors towards a specific action, whether it's signing up for a newsletter, downloading a whitepaper, or making a purchase. This focused approach eliminates distractions and streamlines the user experience, increasing the likelihood of conversion. Moreover, landing pages are tailored to align with specific marketing campaigns, ensuring continuity in messaging and reinforcing the value proposition. By serving as a dedicated destination for prospects, landing pages facilitate targeted communication and enable marketers to track the effectiveness of their efforts with precision.

1. **Focused Messaging**: Landing pages allow marketers to deliver a tailored message that directly addresses the needs and pain points of their target audience. By aligning the content with the corresponding ad or campaign, they create a cohesive journey for visitors, enhancing engagement and fostering trust.

2. **Lead Qualification**: Through strategically placed forms and interactive elements, landing pages enable marketers to gather valuable information about prospects. This data not only facilitates segmentation and personalization but also helps in qualifying leads based on their level of interest and intent.

3. **Measurable Results**: Unlike traditional marketing channels, digital campaigns offer robust analytics capabilities, allowing marketers to track the performance of their

landing pages in real-time. Metrics such as conversion rate, bounce rate, and time on page provide actionable insights that drive optimization efforts and maximize ROI.

3.2 Designing High-Converting Landing Pages with Wishpond

Design plays a crucial role in the success of a landing page. In the crowded online landscape, where attention spans are fleeting, a visually appealing and intuitive layout can make all the difference. Wishpond, a leading marketing platform, offers a suite of tools designed to simplify the process of creating high-converting landing pages.

1. **Intuitive Editor**: Wishpond's drag-and-drop editor empowers marketers to design landing pages without any coding knowledge. With a library of customizable templates and elements, users can easily create visually stunning pages that resonate with their brand identity.

2. **Mobile Optimization**: In an era dominated by smartphones, mobile responsiveness is non-negotiable. Wishpond ensures that landing pages render seamlessly across devices, providing a consistent user experience and maximizing engagement.

3. **Conversion Tools**: From countdown timers to exit-intent pop-ups, Wishpond offers a range of conversion-focused features to captivate visitors and drive action. These tools leverage psychological triggers to nudge prospects towards conversion, whether it's making a purchase or submitting their contact information.

3.3 Optimizing Landing Page Content for Conversions

Content is the cornerstone of any effective landing page. Beyond aesthetics, it's the messaging and copywriting that truly compel visitors to take the desired action. Optimizing content for conversions requires a deep understanding of the target audience, persuasive language, and a keen eye for detail.

1. **Clear Value Proposition**: Within seconds of landing on a page, visitors should understand what's in it for them. A compelling value proposition communicates the benefits of taking action and addresses the pain points of the audience.

2. **Concise Copy**: In the age of information overload, brevity is key. Landing page copy should be concise yet persuasive, focusing on

the most compelling arguments and eliminating any unnecessary fluff.

3. **Compelling Call-to-Action**: The call-to-action (CTA) serves as the lynchpin of a landing page, guiding visitors towards the desired outcome. It should be prominently displayed, action-oriented, and clearly communicate the next steps.

3.4 A/B Testing Your Landing Pages with Wishpond

A/B testing, also known as split testing, is a fundamental practice in conversion rate optimization. By comparing two versions of a landing page and measuring their performance, marketers can identify the elements that resonate most with their audience and iteratively improve their campaigns. Wishpond streamlines the A/B testing process, allowing users to experiment with different headlines, images, CTAs, and more to uncover the winning combination.

1. **Hypothesis Formulation**: Before conducting an A/B test, it's essential to formulate clear hypotheses based on data and insights. Whether it's testing the effectiveness of a headline or the placement of a form, each variation should serve a specific purpose.

2. **Statistical Significance**: A/B testing requires patience and statistical rigor. Marketers must ensure that they collect a sufficient sample size to draw meaningful conclusions and avoid making decisions based on random fluctuations in data.

3. **Iterative Optimization**: A/B testing is not a one-time endeavor but an ongoing process of refinement. By continuously testing and iterating, marketers can uncover new opportunities for improvement and stay ahead of evolving consumer preferences.

3.5 Integrating Landing Pages with Email Marketing

Email marketing remains one of the most effective channels for nurturing leads and driving conversions. By seamlessly integrating landing pages with email campaigns, marketers can create a cohesive user journey that guides prospects from initial interest to eventual conversion.

1. **Lead Capture**: Landing pages serve as the perfect entry point for capturing email addresses and expanding the subscriber list. By offering valuable content or incentives in exchange for contact information, marketers can grow their email database and establish

direct communication channels with prospects.

2. **Personalized Follow-Up**: Once a prospect has submitted their contact information, it's crucial to deliver personalized follow-up emails that reinforce the value proposition and nurture the relationship. By segmenting subscribers based on their interests and behavior, marketers can tailor the content to resonate with each individual.

3. **Conversion Tracking**: Integrating landing pages with email marketing platforms enables seamless tracking of campaign performance and attribution. Marketers can monitor open rates, click-through rates, and conversion metrics to gain insights into the effectiveness of their email campaigns and optimize accordingly.

3.6 Tracking Landing Page Performance Metrics

In the fast-paced world of digital marketing, data is king. Tracking landing page performance metrics not only provides valuable insights into the effectiveness of marketing campaigns but also informs strategic decision-making and optimization efforts.

1. **Conversion Rate**: Perhaps the most critical metric for measuring landing page effectiveness, conversion rate represents the percentage of visitors who take the desired action, whether it's making a purchase, filling out a form, or downloading a resource.

2. **Bounce Rate**: Bounce rate indicates the percentage of visitors who navigate away from the landing page without taking any further action. A high bounce rate may signal issues with page relevance, usability, or messaging that require attention.

3. **Average Time on Page**: The average time spent on a landing page offers insights into visitor engagement and content relevance. A longer average time on page suggests that visitors are actively consuming the content and may be more likely to convert.

4. **Click-Through Rate (CTR)**: For landing pages featuring multiple elements such as CTAs or navigation links, click-through rate measures the percentage of visitors who click on these elements. A high CTR indicates strong engagement and interest in the content.

5. **Return on Investment (ROI)**: Ultimately, the success of a landing page is measured by its contribution to the bottom line. ROI quantifies the financial impact of the landing page in terms of revenue generated or leads acquired, providing a holistic view of its effectiveness.

In conclusion, creating effective landing pages requires a strategic blend of design, content, and optimization techniques. By understanding the importance of landing pages in lead generation, leveraging tools like Wishpond, optimizing content for conversions, conducting A/B tests, integrating with email marketing, and tracking performance metrics, marketers can create compelling experiences that drive results and propel their businesses forward in the digital landscape.

Chapter 4: Mastering Email Marketing with Wishpond

4.1 Building Your Email List with Wishpond

Building an email list is the cornerstone of successful email marketing campaigns, and Wishpond offers a range of tools and strategies to help businesses grow their subscriber base effectively. One key aspect is creating compelling opt-in forms. These forms should be strategically placed on your website, blog posts, and social media profiles to capture visitors' attention and encourage them to subscribe. Wishpond provides customizable templates and advanced targeting options to optimize opt-in form performance.

Another crucial element of list building with Wishpond is leveraging lead magnets. Offering valuable incentives such as eBooks, whitepapers, or exclusive discounts can significantly increase sign-up rates. Wishpond enables businesses to create and deliver lead magnets seamlessly, helping to attract and retain subscribers. Additionally, integrating with other marketing platforms such as CRM systems or social media channels allows for a streamlined approach to capturing leads across various touchpoints.

Moreover, utilizing pop-ups and exit-intent triggers can further enhance list building efforts. Wishpond's tools enable businesses to display pop-ups at strategic moments during a visitor's journey, maximizing the chances of converting them into subscribers. By leveraging exit-intent technology, businesses can capture the attention of visitors who are about to leave the website, presenting them with one last opportunity to subscribe.

4.2 Designing Engaging Email Campaigns

Design plays a pivotal role in the success of email marketing campaigns, as visually appealing and well-structured emails are more likely to capture subscribers' attention and drive desired actions. Wishpond offers a range of features to help businesses design engaging email campaigns that resonate with their audience.

One key aspect is responsive email templates. With Wishpond, businesses can choose from a variety of professionally designed templates that are optimized for mobile devices, ensuring a seamless experience across different screen sizes. Additionally, drag-and-drop editors empower users to customize email templates according to their brand identity and campaign objectives, without the need for coding skills.

Furthermore, dynamic content capabilities enable businesses to personalize email campaigns based on subscriber data and behavior. Wishpond's platform allows for dynamic insertion of content elements such as product recommendations, personalized greetings, or relevant offers, increasing the relevance and effectiveness of email communications.

Another essential feature for designing engaging email campaigns is A/B testing. Wishpond enables businesses to experiment with different elements of their emails, such as subject lines, call-to-action buttons, or imagery, to identify what resonates best with their audience. By analyzing the results of A/B tests, businesses can refine their email campaigns and optimize performance over time.

4.3 Personalizing Email Content with Wishpond

Personalization is a fundamental strategy in email marketing, as it allows businesses to tailor their communications to individual subscribers' preferences, behaviors, and demographics. Wishpond offers robust personalization features to help businesses deliver targeted and relevant content to their audience effectively.

One key aspect of personalization with Wishpond is segmentation. Businesses can segment their email lists based on various criteria such as demographics, purchase history, or engagement levels, allowing for highly targeted and personalized campaigns. By sending tailored content to specific segments, businesses can increase relevance and engagement, ultimately driving better results.

Moreover, dynamic content insertion enables businesses to personalize email content dynamically based on subscriber data. Wishpond's platform allows for the dynamic insertion of content blocks within emails, such as product recommendations, location-specific offers, or personalized messages, ensuring that each subscriber receives a unique and relevant experience.

Additionally, behavioral targeting capabilities enable businesses to personalize email content based on subscribers' past interactions with their brand. Wishpond's platform tracks and analyzes subscriber behavior, allowing businesses to send targeted emails triggered by specific actions or milestones, such as abandoned carts, website visits, or email opens.

4.4 Automating Email Workflows with Wishpond

Email automation is a game-changer for marketers, enabling them to deliver timely and relevant messages to subscribers without manual intervention. Wishpond offers robust automation features that empower businesses to streamline their email workflows and deliver personalized communications at scale.

One key aspect of email automation with Wishpond is workflow automation. Businesses can create automated email sequences or workflows triggered by specific actions or events, such as sign-ups, purchases, or website visits. Wishpond's intuitive workflow builder allows for the creation of complex automation sequences with ease, enabling businesses to nurture leads, onboard new customers, or re-engage inactive subscribers automatically.

Moreover, drip campaigns are a powerful automation tool offered by Wishpond. Businesses can set up drip campaigns to send a series of pre-written emails to subscribers over time, guiding them through the customer journey and nurturing relationships. By delivering relevant content at the right time, drip campaigns help businesses stay top-of-mind and drive conversions.

Additionally, autoresponders enable businesses to send automated responses to subscriber actions or inquiries. Wishpond's platform allows for the customization of autoresponder messages based on triggers such as form submissions, email opens, or link clicks, ensuring timely and personalized communication with subscribers.

4.5 Analyzing Email Campaign Performance

Analyzing email campaign performance is essential for optimizing strategies and driving better results over time. Wishpond offers robust analytics tools that enable businesses to track and measure the effectiveness of their email campaigns comprehensively.

One key aspect of email campaign analysis with Wishpond is tracking key metrics. Businesses can monitor metrics such as open rates, click-through rates, conversion rates, and more to gauge the performance of their email campaigns. Wishpond's analytics dashboard provides real-time insights into campaign performance, allowing businesses to identify trends, patterns, and areas for improvement.

Moreover, split testing capabilities enable businesses to experiment with different elements of their email campaigns to identify what resonates best with their audience. Wishpond's platform allows for A/B testing of various elements such as subject lines, content, calls-to-action, or send times, helping businesses optimize their campaigns for maximum impact.

Additionally, tracking subscriber engagement is crucial for understanding audience preferences and behavior. Wishpond's platform enables businesses to track subscriber engagement metrics such as opens, clicks, and conversions, allowing for a deeper understanding of how subscribers interact with email content. By analyzing engagement data, businesses can tailor their email campaigns to better meet subscribers' needs and preferences.

4.6 Tips for Email Marketing Success with Wishpond

Successfully leveraging Wishpond for email marketing requires a strategic approach and adherence to best practices. Here are some tips to maximize your email marketing success with Wishpond:

- **Define clear goals**: Before launching email campaigns with Wishpond, clearly define your objectives and key performance indicators (KPIs). Whether it's driving sales, increasing brand awareness, or nurturing leads, having clear goals will guide your strategy and measurement efforts.

- **Segment your audience**: Utilize Wishpond's segmentation capabilities to divide your email list into targeted segments based on demographics, behavior, or preferences. By sending personalized content to specific segments, you can increase relevance and engagement.

- **Optimize for mobile**: Ensure that your email campaigns are optimized for mobile devices, as an increasing number of subscribers access their emails on smartphones and tablets. Wishpond's responsive email templates make it easy to create mobile-friendly designs.

- **Test and iterate**: Continuously experiment with different elements of your email campaigns, such as subject lines, content, and send times, using Wishpond's split testing features. Analyze the results and iterate on your approach to improve performance over time.

- **Monitor and analyze**: Regularly monitor the performance of your email campaigns using Wishpond's analytics tools. Track key metrics, identify trends, and adjust your strategy accordingly to maximize results.

By following these tips and leveraging Wishpond's features effectively, you can unlock the full potential of email marketing to engage subscribers, drive conversions, and grow your business.

Chapter 5: Harnessing Social Media for Lead Generation

In today's digital age, social media has become a powerhouse for businesses looking to generate leads and engage with their audience. Leveraging platforms like Wishpond can amplify these efforts, providing tools and strategies to maximize reach and conversions. Let's delve into the various aspects of harnessing social media for lead generation.

5.1 Leveraging Social Media Platforms with Wishpond

Wishpond offers a comprehensive suite of tools designed to seamlessly integrate with various social media platforms, such as Facebook, Instagram, Twitter, and LinkedIn. By leveraging Wishpond's platform, businesses can streamline their lead generation efforts across multiple channels, reaching a wider audience and maximizing their conversion potential.

Points to consider:

- **Multi-channel approach**: Wishpond allows businesses to create campaigns that span across different social media platforms simultaneously, ensuring maximum exposure and engagement.

- **Customizable campaigns**: With Wishpond, businesses can tailor their campaigns to suit the unique characteristics and demographics of each social media platform, optimizing their messaging and content for maximum impact.

- **Unified dashboard**: Wishpond provides a centralized dashboard where businesses can monitor and manage their social media campaigns in real-time, facilitating seamless coordination and optimization.

5.2 Creating Contests and Promotions on Social Media

Contests and promotions are powerful tools for driving engagement and capturing leads on social media. Wishpond enables businesses to effortlessly create and manage various types of contests and promotions, from photo contests to sweepstakes, across different social media platforms.

Points to consider:

- **Lead capture forms**: Wishpond allows businesses to embed lead capture forms directly into their contest pages, enabling them to capture valuable contact information from participants.

- **Viral sharing**: Wishpond's built-in sharing features encourage participants to share the contest with their friends and followers, exponentially increasing its reach and visibility.

- **Automated notifications**: Wishpond automates the process of notifying winners and distributing prizes, saving businesses time and effort while ensuring a smooth and seamless contest experience for participants.

5.3 Integrating Social Media with Your Wishpond Campaigns

Integration is key to maximizing the effectiveness of social media campaigns. Wishpond offers seamless integration with various social media platforms, allowing businesses to leverage the full power of social media within their marketing campaigns.

Points to consider:

- **Social media sharing**: Wishpond enables businesses to easily share their campaigns across multiple social media platforms with just a few clicks, extending their reach and visibility.

- **Social login**: Wishpond allows businesses to implement social login functionality, enabling users to sign up for campaigns using their existing social media accounts, streamlining the registration process and increasing conversion rates.

- **Social media tracking**: Wishpond provides robust tracking and analytics tools that allow businesses to monitor the performance of their social media campaigns in real-time, enabling them to make data-driven decisions and optimize their strategies for maximum effectiveness.

5.4 Engaging with Your Social Media Audience

Engagement is the cornerstone of successful social media lead generation. Wishpond empowers businesses to effectively engage with their social media audience through interactive content, timely responses, and personalized interactions.

Points to consider:

- **Interactive content**: Wishpond enables businesses to create interactive content such as polls, quizzes, and surveys that encourage audience participation and foster engagement.

- **Timely responses**: Wishpond provides tools for managing and responding to comments, messages, and mentions on social media in a timely and efficient manner, fostering positive interactions and building rapport with the audience.

- **Personalized interactions**: Wishpond allows businesses to segment their social media audience based on demographics, interests, and behavior, enabling them to deliver personalized content and messages that resonate with their target audience.

5.5 Analyzing Social Media Metrics with Wishpond

Effective measurement and analysis are essential for optimizing social media campaigns. Wishpond offers robust analytics tools that enable businesses to track and analyze key metrics, gain valuable insights, and make data-driven decisions to improve their lead generation efforts.

Points to consider:

- **Comprehensive reporting**: Wishpond provides detailed reports and dashboards that offer insights into key metrics such as engagement, reach, conversions, and ROI, allowing businesses to track the performance of their social media campaigns and identify areas for improvement.

- **A/B testing**: Wishpond allows businesses to conduct A/B tests to experiment with different campaign elements such as ad copy, visuals, and targeting parameters, helping them identify the most effective strategies for driving engagement and generating leads.

- **Conversion tracking**: Wishpond enables businesses to track the entire customer journey from social media engagement to conversion, providing visibility into which social media channels and campaigns are driving the most leads and revenue.

5.6 Case Studies: Successful Social Media Lead Generation Strategies

Case studies provide valuable insights into real-world examples of successful social media lead generation strategies. Wishpond showcases various case studies that highlight how businesses across different industries have leveraged its platform to achieve remarkable results.

Points to consider:

- **Industry-specific examples**: Wishpond's case studies cover a diverse range of industries, including e-commerce, SaaS, retail, and hospitality, demonstrating the versatility and effectiveness of its platform across various sectors.

- **Quantifiable results**: Wishpond's case studies present concrete metrics and results, such as increased website traffic, lead generation, and revenue growth, showcasing the tangible impact of its platform on businesses' bottom line.

- **Best practices and insights**: Wishpond's case studies offer valuable best practices, tips, and insights gleaned from successful campaigns, providing actionable takeaways that businesses can apply to their own social media lead generation efforts.

In conclusion, harnessing social media for lead generation requires a strategic approach, leveraging the right tools, tactics, and platforms to engage with the audience effectively and drive meaningful results. Wishpond offers a comprehensive suite of solutions that empower businesses to maximize their social media presence, generate quality leads, and achieve their marketing objectives. By leveraging Wishpond's platform and following best practices, businesses can unlock the full potential of social media as a powerful tool for lead generation and business growth.

Chapter 6: Using Wishpond for Marketing Automation

Marketing automation has become a cornerstone for modern businesses aiming to streamline their marketing efforts, engage with their audience effectively, and drive conversions. Among the plethora of tools available, Wishpond stands out as a comprehensive solution offering a myriad of features to automate various aspects of marketing campaigns. In this chapter, we delve into the intricacies of utilizing Wishpond for marketing automation, exploring its capabilities, and uncovering strategies to maximize its potential.

6.1 Understanding Marketing Automation with Wishpond

Marketing automation with Wishpond revolves around the concept of automating repetitive tasks and workflows to streamline marketing processes and enhance efficiency. At its core, Wishpond provides a centralized platform to create, manage, and analyze marketing campaigns across multiple channels such as email, social media, and landing pages. By leveraging automation, businesses can automate lead generation, nurture leads through targeted communication, and ultimately drive conversions.

Key Features of Wishpond for Marketing Automation:

1. **Lead Generation Forms:** Wishpond enables businesses to create customizable lead generation forms embedded seamlessly into their website or landing pages. These forms capture vital information about prospects, allowing businesses to build a robust database of leads.

2. **Email Marketing Automation:** With Wishpond, businesses can design automated email campaigns tailored to different segments of their audience. From welcome emails to drip campaigns, automation streamlines the process of nurturing leads and engaging with customers over time.

3. **Social Media Contests and Promotions:** Wishpond facilitates the creation of interactive social media contests and promotions, driving user engagement and expanding brand reach. Automated features ensure hassle-free management and tracking of contest entries and participant interactions.

4. **Landing Page Optimization:** Wishpond's intuitive interface empowers businesses to

design visually appealing landing pages optimized for conversion. Automated A/B testing capabilities enable continuous refinement and improvement of landing page performance.

6.2 Creating Automated Workflows for Lead Nurturing

Lead nurturing is a critical aspect of the marketing process, aimed at guiding leads through the sales funnel and converting them into loyal customers. Wishpond simplifies the lead nurturing process by allowing businesses to create automated workflows tailored to the unique needs and behaviors of their audience.

Components of Automated Lead Nurturing Workflows:

1. **Trigger Events:** Automated workflows in Wishpond are initiated by trigger events, such as lead form submissions, email opens, or website visits. These trigger events serve as the catalyst for the subsequent actions in the workflow.

2. **Conditional Logic:** Wishpond offers robust conditional logic capabilities, allowing businesses to customize the flow of their

automated workflows based on specific criteria. For example, leads can be segmented based on demographic information, engagement level, or past interactions with the brand.

3. **Multi-channel Engagement:** Automated workflows in Wishpond span multiple channels, including email, social media, and SMS. This omnichannel approach ensures consistent and personalized communication with leads throughout their journey.

4. **Lead Scoring and Qualification:** Wishpond's automation features extend to lead scoring and qualification, enabling businesses to prioritize leads based on their likelihood to convert. By assigning scores to leads based on their engagement level and behavior, businesses can focus their efforts on high-potential prospects.

6.3 Segmenting Your Audience with Wishpond

Segmentation lies at the heart of effective marketing strategies, allowing businesses to target their audience with relevant and personalized content. Wishpond empowers businesses to segment their audience dynamically based on various criteria, enabling more targeted and impactful marketing campaigns.

Methods of Audience Segmentation in Wishpond:

1. **Demographic Segmentation:** Wishpond allows businesses to segment their audience based on demographic attributes such as age, gender, location, and income level. This enables targeted messaging tailored to the specific characteristics of different audience segments.

2. **Behavioral Segmentation:** Behavioral segmentation in Wishpond involves categorizing leads based on their past interactions and behaviors, such as website visits, email opens, and social media engagement. By understanding how leads interact with their brand, businesses can deliver personalized content and offers.

3. **Lifecycle Stage Segmentation:** Wishpond facilitates segmentation based on the lifecycle stage of leads, from awareness to consideration to decision. This enables businesses to deliver relevant content and offers tailored to where leads are in their buying journey.

4. **Custom Tags and Attributes:** Wishpond allows businesses to create custom tags and attributes to further refine audience segmentation. Whether it's tagging leads based on their interests or purchase history, custom tags provide additional flexibility in targeting specific audience segments.

6.4 Personalizing Customer Journeys with Automation

Personalization is key to creating meaningful interactions with customers and building lasting relationships. Wishpond enables businesses to personalize customer journeys through targeted communication, tailored offers, and timely engagement, all powered by automation.

Strategies for Personalizing Customer Journeys with Wishpond:

1. **Dynamic Content Personalization:** Wishpond's automation features enable the dynamic personalization of content based on individual preferences and behaviors. By delivering content that resonates with each customer's interests and needs, businesses can enhance engagement and drive conversions.

2. **Behavior-based Triggers:** Wishpond allows businesses to set up behavior-based triggers that automatically deliver relevant messages or offers based on specific actions taken by customers. Whether it's a cart abandonment email or a personalized recommendation based on browsing history, automation ensures timely and personalized communication.

3. **Segment-specific Campaigns:** Wishpond facilitates the creation of segment-specific campaigns tailored to the unique characteristics of different audience segments. By crafting campaigns that resonate with the interests and preferences of each segment, businesses can foster deeper connections with their customers.

4. **Integration with CRM Data:** Wishpond seamlessly integrates with CRM systems, enabling businesses to leverage customer data to personalize interactions. By syncing customer information across platforms, businesses can deliver highly targeted and personalized experiences at every touchpoint.

6.5 Integrating Wishpond with CRM Systems

CRM systems play a pivotal role in managing customer relationships and facilitating seamless communication between businesses and their customers. Wishpond offers seamless integration with leading CRM platforms, empowering businesses to leverage customer data and streamline their marketing efforts.

Benefits of Integrating Wishpond with CRM Systems:

1. **Unified Customer Profiles:** Integration with CRM systems enables businesses to maintain a centralized repository of customer data, including contact information, purchase history, and interaction logs. This unified view of customer profiles ensures consistency and accuracy in marketing campaigns.

2. **Automated Data Syncing:** Wishpond's integration with CRM systems automates the syncing of customer data, ensuring that marketing campaigns are always based on the latest and most relevant information. This eliminates manual data entry tasks and reduces the risk of errors.

3. **Enhanced Targeting and Segmentation:** By combining Wishpond's segmentation capabilities with CRM data, businesses can create highly targeted and personalized marketing campaigns. Whether it's targeting high-value customers or re-engaging dormant leads, integration with CRM systems unlocks new possibilities for segmentation.

4. **Closed-loop Reporting:** Integration with CRM systems enables closed-loop reporting, allowing businesses to track the impact of their marketing efforts on sales and revenue. By connecting marketing activities to actual business outcomes, businesses can measure ROI more effectively and optimize their strategies accordingly.

6.6 Monitoring and Optimizing Marketing Automation Performance

Continuous monitoring and optimization are essential for maximizing the effectiveness of marketing automation efforts. Wishpond provides robust analytics and reporting tools to track the performance of marketing campaigns, identify areas for improvement, and optimize strategies for better results.

Metrics to Monitor and Optimize in Wishpond:

1. **Email Engagement Metrics:** Wishpond's email marketing automation features provide insights into key engagement metrics such as open rates, click-through rates, and conversion rates. Monitoring these metrics allows businesses to identify which emails resonate with their audience and optimize future campaigns accordingly.

2. **Lead Nurturing Effectiveness:** By tracking the progression of leads through automated workflows, businesses can gauge the effectiveness of their lead nurturing efforts. Metrics such as lead conversion rates and time to conversion provide valuable insights into the performance of automated workflows.

3. **Campaign ROI:** Wishpond's reporting tools enable businesses to track the ROI of their marketing campaigns, including both automated and manual efforts. By comparing campaign costs to generated revenue, businesses can assess the overall effectiveness and profitability of their marketing automation initiatives.

4. **Segmentation Performance:** Monitoring the performance of audience segmentation allows businesses to evaluate the relevance and

effectiveness of their targeted campaigns. Analyzing metrics such as engagement rates and conversion rates across different segments helps optimize segmentation strategies for maximum impact.

In conclusion, Wishpond offers a comprehensive suite of features for marketing automation, empowering businesses to streamline their marketing efforts, personalize customer experiences, and drive measurable results. By understanding the capabilities of Wishpond and implementing best practices for marketing automation, businesses can unlock new opportunities for growth and success in today's competitive landscape.

Chapter 7: Optimizing Conversions with Wishpond

In the realm of digital marketing, conversion optimization stands as a pivotal strategy, often making the difference between success and failure for businesses striving to thrive online. Within this landscape, Wishpond emerges as a comprehensive toolset, offering a myriad of features designed to enhance conversion rates and drive growth. Let's delve into the intricacies of optimizing conversions with Wishpond, exploring its significance, tracking tools, A/B testing capabilities, user behavior analysis, insights for funnel improvement, and real-world case studies exemplifying its efficacy.

7.1 The Importance of Conversion Optimization

Conversion optimization isn't merely an option; it's the lifeblood of online businesses, fueling growth and profitability. At its core, conversion optimization revolves around the art and science of persuading website visitors to take desired actions, whether it's making a purchase, signing up for a newsletter, or filling out a contact form. Every click, every scroll, every interaction presents an opportunity to guide users along the conversion path. By refining various elements of a website, such as design, copy, and user experience, businesses can systematically increase their conversion rates, translating into tangible business outcomes like higher revenue, improved ROI, and enhanced customer satisfaction.

Successful conversion optimization hinges on a deep understanding of target audiences, meticulous analysis of user behavior, and continuous experimentation to fine-tune strategies. It's a dynamic process that demands agility and adaptability, as consumer preferences and market trends evolve incessantly. With Wishpond, businesses gain access to a suite of tools tailored to streamline and optimize this process, empowering them to unlock their full conversion potential.

7.2 Using Wishpond's Conversion Tracking Tools

Wishpond's conversion tracking tools serve as the cornerstone of effective optimization efforts, providing businesses with invaluable insights into the performance of their marketing campaigns and website interactions. By meticulously tracking key metrics such as click-through rates, conversion rates, bounce rates, and customer journeys, Wishpond enables businesses to identify areas of strength and weakness within their conversion funnels.

One of the standout features of Wishpond's tracking tools is its seamless integration with various digital platforms, including websites, social media channels, and email marketing campaigns. This holistic approach enables businesses to gain a comprehensive view of their marketing ecosystem, allowing for informed decision-making and targeted optimizations. Whether it's monitoring the effectiveness of Facebook ads, analyzing email engagement metrics, or tracking conversions across different landing pages, Wishpond equips businesses with the data-driven insights needed to drive meaningful results.

Furthermore, Wishpond's tracking tools offer granular segmentation capabilities, allowing businesses to segment their audience based on demographics, behaviors, and engagement levels. This level of granularity enables hyper-targeted marketing efforts, ensuring that messages resonate with the right audience at the right time, thus maximizing conversion potential.

7.3 Implementing A/B Testing for Conversion Rate Optimization

A/B testing, also known as split testing, lies at the heart of conversion rate optimization, serving as a systematic approach to iteratively improve website performance. By comparing two or more versions of a webpage, email, or advertisement, businesses can pinpoint which elements resonate most with their audience and drive higher conversion rates.

Wishpond simplifies the A/B testing process with its intuitive interface and robust experimentation capabilities. From testing different headlines and calls-to-action to evaluating the impact of design variations and pricing strategies, Wishpond empowers businesses to make data-driven decisions and optimize their conversion funnels for maximum impact.

When implementing A/B tests with Wishpond, businesses should adhere to best practices to ensure meaningful results. Firstly, it's essential to clearly define objectives and hypotheses for each experiment, outlining the specific metrics that will be measured and the expected outcomes. Secondly, businesses should ensure that tests are conducted on a statistically significant sample size to mitigate the risk of false positives or misleading conclusions. Finally, continuous monitoring and iteration are key to unlocking the full potential of A/B testing, as consumer preferences and market dynamics evolve over time.

7.4 Analyzing User Behavior with Wishpond

Understanding user behavior is paramount to effective conversion optimization, as it provides invaluable insights into the motivations, preferences, and pain points of website visitors. Wishpond's user behavior analysis tools offer a comprehensive suite of features designed to unravel the complexities of user interactions and inform strategic decision-making.

By leveraging advanced analytics and tracking technologies, Wishpond enables businesses to gain deep insights into how users navigate their websites, where they encounter friction points, and what influences their purchasing decisions. From heatmaps and click tracking to session recordings and form analytics, Wishpond equips businesses with the tools needed to visualize and understand user behavior at every touchpoint.

One of the key advantages of Wishpond's user behavior analysis tools is their ability to uncover actionable insights in real-time, allowing businesses to identify and address issues promptly. Whether it's optimizing website layout for better usability, refining product messaging to resonate with target audiences, or streamlining checkout processes to reduce friction, Wishpond empowers businesses to make data-driven optimizations that drive tangible results.

7.5 Improving Conversion Funnels with Wishpond Insights

Conversion funnels serve as a roadmap for guiding users from initial engagement to final conversion, making them a critical component of any conversion optimization strategy. Wishpond Insights offers businesses a comprehensive toolkit for optimizing their conversion funnels, enabling them to identify bottlenecks, capitalize on opportunities, and streamline the customer journey for maximum efficiency.

With Wishpond Insights, businesses can visualize their conversion funnels from end to end, tracking user progression through each stage of the customer lifecycle. By analyzing drop-off points, conversion rates, and user behavior patterns, businesses can pinpoint areas of friction and implement targeted interventions to improve funnel performance.

Moreover, Wishpond Insights goes beyond basic funnel visualization, offering advanced features such as cohort analysis, predictive modeling, and funnel segmentation. These capabilities enable businesses to gain a deeper understanding of their audience segments, predict future behavior trends, and tailor their conversion strategies accordingly.

By leveraging Wishpond Insights, businesses can unlock the full potential of their conversion funnels, driving higher engagement, increased conversions, and improved customer satisfaction.

7.6 Case Studies: Successful Conversion Optimization Strategies

While theoretical frameworks and best practices provide valuable guidance, real-world case studies offer tangible proof of concept, showcasing the transformative power of conversion optimization strategies. Wishpond boasts a diverse portfolio of case studies highlighting successful optimization initiatives across various industries and business models.

One such case study revolves around an e-commerce retailer struggling to convert website visitors into paying customers. By leveraging Wishpond's suite of conversion optimization tools, including A/B testing, user behavior analysis, and funnel insights, the retailer was able to identify friction points in the customer journey, optimize product pages for better usability, and personalize messaging to resonate with target audiences. The result? A significant increase in conversion rates, revenue growth, and customer satisfaction.

In another case study, a B2B SaaS company sought to improve the performance of its lead generation efforts. Through rigorous A/B testing of landing pages, email campaigns, and lead magnets, coupled with in-depth analysis of user behavior and funnel insights, the company was able to refine its targeting strategies, optimize conversion pathways, and increase lead quality. The outcome? A substantial uptick in lead conversion rates, shortened sales cycles, and enhanced marketing ROI.

These case studies underscore the transformative impact of conversion optimization when implemented strategically and supported by robust tools and analytics. By embracing a data-driven approach to optimization and continuously iterating on strategies based on real-world insights, businesses can unlock untapped growth opportunities and propel their digital success.

This exploration delves deep into the realm of conversion optimization with Wishpond, unraveling its multifaceted approach to driving growth and maximizing conversion potential. From tracking tools and A/B testing capabilities to user behavior analysis and funnel insights, Wishpond offers a comprehensive toolkit for businesses seeking to thrive in the competitive landscape of digital marketing. Through real-world case studies, we witness firsthand the transformative power of conversion optimization when coupled with strategic implementation and data-driven decision-making.

Chapter 8: Scaling Your Lead Generation Efforts

Lead generation is the lifeblood of any business aiming for growth and sustainability. In today's digital landscape, where competition is fierce and attention spans are fleeting, scaling lead generation efforts becomes paramount. In this chapter, we delve into various strategies, tools, and trends that can help businesses scale their lead generation effectively, with a particular focus on leveraging Wishpond's platform for optimal results.

8.1 Strategies for Scaling Lead Generation with Wishpond

Wishpond offers a plethora of features and tools tailored for lead generation across multiple channels. From customizable landing pages to intuitive email marketing automation, the platform equips businesses with the essentials to expand their reach and capture leads at every touchpoint.

1. **Optimized Landing Pages**: Wishpond enables users to create visually appealing and conversion-focused landing pages without the need for extensive coding knowledge. With drag-and-drop functionality and a library of templates, businesses can quickly deploy

landing pages tailored to specific campaigns or target demographics.

2. **Social Media Contests and Promotions**: Leveraging Wishpond's social media integration, businesses can run contests, giveaways, and promotions to engage their audience and generate leads organically. By incentivizing participation and sharing, brands can amplify their reach and attract new prospects effectively.

3. **Email Marketing Automation**: Wishpond streamlines the process of nurturing leads through automated email sequences. By segmenting leads based on behavior, demographics, or engagement level, businesses can deliver personalized content that resonates with their audience, ultimately driving conversions and sales.

4. **Lead Tracking and Analytics**: With Wishpond's robust analytics dashboard, businesses can track the performance of their lead generation efforts in real-time. From conversion rates to campaign ROI, granular insights empower businesses to optimize their strategies and allocate resources effectively.

8.2 Expanding Your Reach with Wishpond's Growth Tools

Scaling lead generation requires expanding reach across various online channels and touchpoints. Wishpond's growth tools provide businesses with the means to extend their digital footprint and engage prospects wherever they may be.

1. **Social Media Publishing and Scheduling**: Wishpond simplifies social media management by enabling users to schedule posts across multiple platforms in advance. By maintaining a consistent presence and sharing valuable content, businesses can attract followers, drive traffic, and generate leads from social channels.

2. **Website Pop-ups and Forms**: Wishpond offers customizable pop-ups and forms that can be strategically placed on websites to capture visitor information and convert them into leads. Whether it's an exit-intent pop-up or a timed overlay, these tools help maximize lead generation potential and minimize bounce rates.

3. **Referral Programs**: Encouraging existing customers or subscribers to refer their friends and colleagues can be a powerful driver of

lead generation. Wishpond facilitates the setup and management of referral programs, incentivizing referrals with discounts, rewards, or exclusive content.

4. **SEO and Content Marketing**: Wishpond provides SEO tools and content management capabilities to help businesses improve their online visibility and attract organic traffic. By optimizing website content, publishing blog posts, and implementing keyword strategies, businesses can attract qualified leads from search engines.

8.3 Collaborating with Partners for Joint Lead Generation Campaigns

Collaborating with complementary businesses or industry partners can amplify lead generation efforts and unlock new opportunities for growth. Wishpond facilitates seamless collaboration through its partnership features and integrations.

1. **Cross-Promotional Campaigns**: Partnering with non-competing businesses to co-create and promote joint campaigns can expand reach and introduce brands to new audiences. Wishpond's collaboration tools make it easy to coordinate efforts, track referrals, and

mutually benefit from shared lead generation initiatives.

2. **Affiliate Marketing Programs**: Establishing an affiliate marketing program with influencers, bloggers, or industry experts can drive targeted traffic and generate high-quality leads. Wishpond's affiliate tracking and management capabilities simplify the process of recruiting, tracking, and rewarding affiliates for their contributions.

3. **Event Sponsorship and Participation**: Sponsoring or participating in industry events, conferences, or webinars presents opportunities to connect with prospects and capture leads in a more targeted setting. Wishpond's event management tools can help businesses streamline registration, engagement, and follow-up processes for maximum impact.

4. **Co-Branded Content and Resources**: Collaborating on the creation of co-branded content such as eBooks, webinars, or case studies can provide valuable assets for lead generation and thought leadership. Wishpond's content collaboration features facilitate the creation, distribution, and

promotion of co-branded content to engage prospects and drive conversions.

8.4 Leveraging Paid Advertising with Wishpond

While organic methods are essential for sustainable lead generation, paid advertising can provide a significant boost in reach and visibility, especially in competitive markets. Wishpond offers robust features for managing and optimizing paid advertising campaigns across various platforms.

1. **Facebook and Instagram Ads**: Wishpond's integration with Facebook Ads Manager enables businesses to create, launch, and track advertising campaigns directly from the platform. With advanced targeting options and ad formats, businesses can reach specific demographics, retarget website visitors, and generate leads efficiently.

2. **Google Ads and Remarketing**: Wishpond's Google Ads integration empowers businesses to leverage the power of search advertising and display remarketing to capture leads at

different stages of the buyer's journey. By bidding on relevant keywords and targeting users based on their online behavior, businesses can maximize ROI and drive conversions.

3. **LinkedIn Advertising**: For B2B businesses targeting professionals and decision-makers, Wishpond's integration with LinkedIn Ads provides access to a highly targeted advertising platform. From sponsored content to InMail campaigns, businesses can reach key stakeholders and generate quality leads within their niche or industry.

4. **Ad Performance Tracking and Optimization**: Wishpond's ad tracking and analytics tools enable businesses to monitor the performance of their paid advertising campaigns in real-time. By analyzing metrics such as click-through rates, conversion rates, and cost-per-acquisition, businesses can optimize their ad spend and maximize ROI for sustainable lead generation.

8.5 Monitoring and Adjusting Your Scaling Strategies

Scaling lead generation is an iterative process that requires continuous monitoring, analysis, and adjustment. Wishpond offers comprehensive reporting and optimization features to help businesses refine their strategies and adapt to changing market dynamics.

1. **A/B Testing and Optimization**: Wishpond allows users to conduct A/B tests on various elements of their lead generation campaigns, including landing pages, email subject lines, and ad creatives. By testing different variables and measuring performance, businesses can identify winning strategies and optimize for maximum conversions.

2. **Conversion Funnel Analysis**: Understanding the customer journey and identifying potential bottlenecks in the conversion funnel is essential for optimizing lead generation efforts. Wishpond's funnel analytics tools provide insights into user behavior at each stage of the funnel, allowing businesses to pinpoint areas for improvement and enhance overall conversion rates.

3. **Lead Scoring and Qualification**: Wishpond's lead scoring capabilities enable businesses to prioritize leads based on their likelihood to convert or engage with the brand. By assigning scores based on demographics,

behavior, and engagement level, businesses can focus their resources on high-value prospects and improve sales efficiency.

4. **CRM Integration and Follow-Up**: Seamless integration with CRM platforms allows businesses to synchronize lead data and streamline follow-up processes. Wishpond enables automated lead nurturing, follow-up emails, and task reminders to ensure that no lead falls through the cracks and that every opportunity is maximized.

8.6 Future Trends in Lead Generation and Wishpond's Role

As technology continues to evolve and consumer behaviors shift, the landscape of lead generation is constantly evolving. Wishpond remains at the forefront of innovation, anticipating future trends and equipping businesses with the tools and insights needed to stay ahead of the curve.

1. **AI and Predictive Analytics**: The integration of artificial intelligence and predictive analytics holds immense potential for optimizing lead generation processes. Wishpond is exploring ways to leverage AI algorithms to analyze vast amounts of data, predict customer behavior, and personalize

lead generation strategies for maximum impact.

2. **Interactive Content and Experiences**: Interactive content formats such as quizzes, polls, and interactive videos are gaining popularity as they offer immersive and engaging experiences for prospects. Wishpond is investing in interactive content creation tools to help businesses captivate audiences and drive meaningful interactions that lead to conversions.

3. **Chatbots and Conversational Marketing**: Chatbots are becoming increasingly sophisticated in their ability to engage and qualify leads in real-time through conversational marketing. Wishpond is developing chatbot integrations to enable businesses to automate lead capture, qualification, and support processes, delivering personalized experiences at scale.

4. **Privacy and Data Compliance**: With growing concerns around data privacy and compliance regulations such as GDPR and CCPA, businesses must prioritize transparency and consent in their lead generation practices. Wishpond is enhancing its platform with

features for managing consent, data encryption, and compliance reporting to help businesses build trust and maintain compliance with evolving regulations.

In conclusion, scaling lead generation requires a multifaceted approach that encompasses strategic planning, tactical execution, and continuous optimization. Wishpond offers a comprehensive suite of tools and features designed to empower businesses to expand their reach, engage prospects effectively, and drive sustainable growth in an ever-changing digital landscape. By embracing innovation, collaboration, and data-driven insights, businesses can unlock new opportunities and stay ahead of the curve in lead generation excellence.

Chapter 9: Troubleshooting Common Issues with Wishpond

Wishpond, like any comprehensive marketing platform, can encounter a myriad of issues that can impede its effectiveness. From technical glitches to low conversion rates and integration challenges, troubleshooting these problems requires a systematic approach and a deep understanding of the platform's functionalities. In this chapter, we'll delve into the common stumbling blocks faced by Wishpond users and explore effective strategies for identifying, addressing, and preventing them.

9.1 Identifying and Resolving Technical Issues

Technical issues can arise unexpectedly, disrupting marketing campaigns and causing frustration for both marketers and customers. Common technical glitches with Wishpond may include slow loading times, form submission errors, or issues with tracking pixels. To effectively identify and resolve these issues, it's essential to conduct thorough diagnostics.

1. **Diagnostic Checklist**: Begin by systematically checking each component of your Wishpond setup, including landing pages, forms, email automation sequences, and integrations. Look

for any error messages, inconsistencies in data tracking, or performance discrepancies.

- **Landing Pages**: Ensure that all elements, such as images, videos, and CTAs, are loading correctly across various devices and browsers.

- **Forms**: Test form submissions to verify that data is captured accurately and that autoresponders or email notifications are triggered promptly.

- **Email Automation**: Review the status of scheduled email campaigns and confirm that emails are being delivered to the intended recipients without delays or errors.

- **Integrations**: Check the connectivity of third-party integrations, such as CRM systems or payment gateways, to identify any synchronization issues.

2. **Error Logs and Reports**: Utilize Wishpond's built-in error logging and reporting features to pinpoint specific issues and track their frequency and impact over time. Analyzing error logs can provide valuable insights into

recurring patterns or underlying system failures that require immediate attention.

3. **Customer Feedback and Support Tickets**: Pay close attention to user feedback and support tickets related to technical issues. Users often report issues that may not be immediately apparent through internal diagnostics, offering valuable perspectives on usability and performance issues.

4. **Collaboration with Technical Support**: If you encounter technical challenges that cannot be resolved internally, don't hesitate to reach out to Wishpond's technical support team for assistance. Provide detailed information about the issue, including steps to reproduce it, screenshots, and any relevant error codes or messages.

By following a systematic diagnostic approach and leveraging available resources, you can effectively identify and resolve technical issues that may arise within the Wishpond platform, ensuring seamless operation and optimal performance for your marketing campaigns.

9.2 Addressing Low Conversion Rates

Low conversion rates are a common concern for marketers using Wishpond to drive leads and sales. Whether it's landing page visitors failing to complete a form or email subscribers not engaging with promotional offers, addressing low conversion rates requires a combination of data analysis, optimization strategies, and experimentation.

1. **Conversion Funnel Analysis**: Start by analyzing the various stages of your conversion funnel, from initial lead acquisition to final conversion actions. Identify potential bottlenecks or drop-off points where prospects are abandoning the conversion process.

2. **A/B Testing and Optimization**: Implement A/B testing experiments to identify factors that influence conversion rates, such as headline variations, CTA design, form length, or offer incentives. Continuously optimize your landing pages, email content, and advertising campaigns based on insights gained from experimentation.

3. **Audience Segmentation and Personalization**: Segment your audience based on demographics, behavior, or

engagement history, and tailor your marketing messages and offers to address their specific needs and preferences. Personalization can significantly improve conversion rates by making your communications more relevant and compelling to individual recipients.

4. **Clear Value Proposition and Call-to-Action**: Ensure that your value proposition is clearly communicated across all marketing touchpoints, highlighting the benefits of your products or services and addressing potential objections. Use persuasive CTAs that prompt immediate action and create a sense of urgency or scarcity.

5. **Performance Tracking and Analytics**: Regularly monitor key performance indicators (KPIs) related to conversion rates, such as click-through rates, form submission rates, and purchase conversion rates. Use analytics tools within Wishpond to track user interactions and identify areas for improvement.

By systematically analyzing your conversion funnel, testing optimization strategies, and refining your messaging and targeting approach, you can effectively address low conversion rates and improve the overall performance of your marketing campaigns with Wishpond.

9.3 Dealing with Deliverability Problems in Email Marketing

Email deliverability issues can significantly impact the success of your email marketing campaigns, leading to low open rates, high bounce rates, and potential damage to your sender reputation. To mitigate deliverability problems within Wishpond's email marketing module, consider the following strategies:

1. **Maintain List Hygiene**: Regularly clean your email lists to remove invalid or inactive email addresses, spam traps, and subscribers who have not engaged with your emails for an extended period. Maintaining list hygiene improves deliverability rates and reduces the risk of being flagged as spam.

2. **Authenticate Your Domain**: Configure domain authentication settings, such as SPF, DKIM, and DMARC, to verify the authenticity of your email communications and enhance your sender reputation. Authenticating your domain helps prevent spoofing and phishing attempts, increasing the likelihood of inbox placement.

3. **Optimize Email Content**: Craft engaging and relevant email content that resonates with your audience and encourages interaction. Avoid using spammy language, excessive punctuation, or deceptive subject lines that may trigger spam filters or deter recipients from opening your emails.

4. **Monitor Sender Reputation**: Monitor your sender reputation using tools like Sender Score or Return Path to track your email sending reputation and identify any issues that may affect deliverability. Address any red flags, such as high spam complaint rates or blacklisting, promptly to maintain a positive sender reputation.

5. **Comply with Regulations**: Ensure compliance with email marketing regulations, such as the CAN-SPAM Act or GDPR, by providing clear opt-in mechanisms, honoring unsubscribe requests promptly, and respecting recipients' preferences and privacy rights. Non-compliance can result in legal consequences and damage to your brand reputation.

By implementing these deliverability best practices and staying vigilant about monitoring and maintaining your email infrastructure, you can maximize the effectiveness of your email marketing efforts within the Wishpond platform and achieve better inbox placement and engagement rates.

9.4 Overcoming Integration Challenges

Integrating Wishpond with other marketing tools, CRMs, or e-commerce platforms is essential for streamlining workflows and maximizing the value of your marketing stack. However, integration challenges can arise due to compatibility issues, data synchronization errors, or API limitations. To overcome these challenges, consider the following strategies:

1. **Choose Compatible Integrations**: Select integrations that are compatible with Wishpond's API and support seamless data exchange between systems. Research integration options thoroughly and prioritize solutions that offer robust documentation, reliable support, and proven compatibility with Wishpond.

2. **Custom Integration Development**: If pre-built integrations do not meet your specific requirements, consider developing custom integration solutions using Wishpond's API or third-party middleware platforms. Custom

integrations allow you to tailor data flows and functionality to align with your unique business processes.

3. **Data Mapping and Synchronization**: Define clear data mapping rules and synchronization protocols to ensure consistency and accuracy when transferring data between Wishpond and other systems. Establishing standardized data formats and field mappings minimizes the risk of data loss or corruption during integration processes.

4. **Testing and Validation**: Thoroughly test integration workflows in a controlled environment to identify any potential issues or discrepancies before deploying them in a production environment. Validate data integrity and functionality at each stage of the integration process to mitigate risks and ensure seamless operation.

5. **Continuous Monitoring and Maintenance**: Regularly monitor integration performance and data flows to detect and address any anomalies or errors promptly. Implement monitoring tools and alerts to notify stakeholders of integration failures or data discrepancies in real-time, enabling swift

resolution and preventing disruptions to marketing operations.

By adopting a systematic approach to integration planning, development, and maintenance, you can overcome common challenges and achieve seamless interoperability between Wishpond and your existing marketing ecosystem, maximizing efficiency and ROI.

9.5 Handling Customer Support and Feedback

Effective customer support and feedback management are crucial for maintaining customer satisfaction and loyalty within the Wishpond platform. Whether users encounter technical issues, have questions about platform features, or wish to provide feedback on their user experience, responsive and knowledgeable support is essential.

1. **Multichannel Support**: Offer multiple channels for users to seek assistance and provide feedback, such as email support, live chat, knowledge base articles, and community forums. Cater to different communication preferences and ensure prompt responses across all channels to minimize user frustration.

2. **Knowledge Base and Self-Service Resources**: Develop a comprehensive

knowledge base containing FAQs, troubleshooting guides, and video tutorials to empower users to troubleshoot common issues independently. Provide intuitive search functionality and regularly update content to reflect changes and new feature releases.

3. **Ticketing System and SLA Management**: Implement a robust ticketing system to track and prioritize support requests efficiently. Define service level agreements (SLAs) for response times and resolution targets, setting clear expectations for users and ensuring timely resolution of support issues.

4. **Feedback Collection and Analysis**: Solicit feedback from users through surveys, feedback forms, or in-app feedback prompts to gather insights into their satisfaction levels, pain points, and feature requests. Analyze feedback data systematically to identify recurring themes or areas for improvement and prioritize initiatives accordingly.

5. **Continuous Improvement Initiatives**: Continuously iterate and improve your customer support processes based on feedback and performance metrics. Invest in training and development for support staff,

implement automation and self-service solutions where feasible, and foster a culture of customer-centricity throughout the organization.

By prioritizing proactive support measures, leveraging user feedback to drive continuous improvement, and fostering a customer-centric culture, you can effectively manage customer support and feedback within the Wishpond platform, enhancing user satisfaction and retention.

9.6 Tips for Preventing Future Issues

Prevention is often the best strategy for mitigating common issues and maintaining the long-term reliability and effectiveness of your Wishpond marketing campaigns. Consider implementing the following tips to proactively prevent future issues:

1. **Regular Platform Updates and Maintenance**: Stay up-to-date with platform updates, bug fixes, and security patches provided by Wishpond. Schedule regular maintenance windows to perform system checks, database optimizations, and platform upgrades to keep your environment running smoothly.

2. **Documentation and Training**: Provide comprehensive documentation, training materials, and onboarding resources for users to familiarize themselves with Wishpond's features, best practices, and troubleshooting guidelines. Empower users to leverage the platform effectively and minimize reliance on support resources.

3. **Proactive Monitoring and Alerts**: Implement monitoring tools and automated alerts to proactively detect and address potential issues before they escalate. Monitor key performance indicators, system health metrics, and user feedback trends to identify emerging issues and take preemptive action.

4. **Quality Assurance Testing**: Conduct thorough quality assurance testing for new campaigns, features, or integrations before deploying them to production environments. Test functionality, performance, and compatibility across various devices, browsers, and user scenarios to ensure a seamless user experience.

5. **Collaborative Problem-Solving Culture**: Foster a culture of collaboration and knowledge sharing among marketing teams,

technical staff, and support personnel. Encourage open communication, peer mentoring, and cross-functional teamwork to facilitate swift problem resolution and continuous improvement.

By proactively implementing preventive measures and fostering a culture of collaboration and continuous improvement, you can minimize the occurrence of common issues and ensure the long-term success of your marketing initiatives within the Wishpond platform.

In conclusion, troubleshooting common issues with Wishpond requires a combination of technical expertise, data analysis, and proactive problem-solving. By following systematic diagnostic procedures, optimizing conversion strategies, addressing deliverability challenges, overcoming integration hurdles, managing customer support effectively, and implementing preventive measures, you can maximize the reliability, effectiveness, and ROI of your Wishpond marketing campaigns.

Chapter 10: Measuring Success and ROI with Wishpond

In the dynamic world of digital marketing, understanding the efficacy of your campaigns is paramount. With Wishpond, a robust marketing automation platform, businesses gain invaluable insights into their lead generation efforts, allowing them to gauge success, track ROI, and refine strategies for optimal performance. This chapter delves into various aspects of measuring success and ROI with Wishpond, encompassing the definition of key performance indicators (KPIs), tracking and analyzing metrics, calculating ROI, reporting to stakeholders, iterating strategies, and setting new goals.

10.1 Defining Key Performance Indicators (KPIs) for Lead Generation

The foundation of any successful marketing endeavor lies in setting clear and relevant KPIs. When it comes to lead generation, identifying the metrics that truly matter can be a nuanced process. Wishpond empowers businesses to define KPIs tailored to their specific objectives, whether it's increasing website traffic, boosting conversion rates, or nurturing leads through the sales funnel.

In delineating KPIs for lead generation, several factors come into play:

- **Conversion Rate:** Measure the percentage of website visitors who take the desired action, such as filling out a contact form or downloading a resource.

- **Lead Quality:** Assess the quality of leads generated by evaluating factors like demographics, engagement level, and likelihood to convert.

- **Cost per Lead (CPL):** Calculate the average cost incurred to acquire a single lead, factoring in expenses related to advertising, content creation, and lead nurturing efforts.

- **Lead Velocity:** Track the rate at which new leads are entering the system, providing insights into the scalability and growth potential of your lead generation efforts.

- **Customer Acquisition Cost (CAC):** Determine the cost associated with acquiring a new customer, considering all marketing and sales expenses incurred throughout the customer journey.

By aligning KPIs with overarching business goals, organizations can effectively measure the success of their lead generation initiatives and make data-driven decisions to optimize performance.

10.2 Tracking and Analyzing Metrics with Wishpond Analytics

With Wishpond's comprehensive analytics suite, businesses gain access to a treasure trove of data to track and analyze the performance of their marketing campaigns. From website traffic and email open rates to conversion funnels and social media engagement, Wishpond provides a plethora of metrics to paint a holistic picture of your lead generation efforts.

Key features of Wishpond Analytics include:

- **Real-time Monitoring:** Monitor campaign performance in real-time, allowing for timely interventions and adjustments to maximize results.

- **Conversion Funnel Analysis:** Visualize the customer journey from initial touchpoint to conversion, identifying potential bottlenecks and optimizing the funnel for improved efficiency.

- **A/B Testing:** Experiment with different elements of your campaigns, such as ad copy, imagery, and call-to-action buttons, to identify the most effective variations.

- **Attribution Modeling:** Attribute conversions to specific marketing channels and touchpoints, enabling a more accurate assessment of ROI and resource allocation.

By leveraging Wishpond Analytics, marketers can gain actionable insights into their lead generation efforts, identify areas for improvement, and refine strategies to drive better results.

10.3 Calculating Return on Investment (ROI) for Wishpond Campaigns

Determining the ROI of marketing campaigns is essential for assessing their effectiveness and justifying investment decisions. Wishpond simplifies the process of calculating ROI by providing robust tools for tracking expenses and attributing conversions to specific campaigns.

To calculate ROI for Wishpond campaigns, follow these steps:

1. **Identify Campaign Costs:** Sum up all expenses associated with the campaign, including advertising spend, content creation costs, and platform subscription fees.

2. **Track Conversions:** Utilize Wishpond's tracking capabilities to attribute conversions to the respective campaigns, distinguishing between leads generated and actual customers acquired.

3. **Calculate Revenue Generated:** Quantify the revenue generated as a result of the campaign, taking into account the lifetime value of acquired customers and the associated sales revenue.

4. **Compute ROI:** Use the formula [(Revenue Generated - Campaign Costs) / Campaign Costs] * 100 to calculate the ROI percentage.

By diligently tracking expenses and attributing conversions, businesses can accurately assess the ROI of their Wishpond campaigns, enabling informed decision-making and resource allocation.

10.4 Reporting on Lead Generation Success to Stakeholders

Effective communication with stakeholders is essential for garnering support, demonstrating value, and fostering alignment with organizational objectives. Wishpond equips marketers with intuitive reporting tools to convey the success of lead generation efforts in a clear and compelling manner.

When reporting on lead generation success to stakeholders, consider the following tips:

- **Focus on Key Metrics:** Highlight key performance indicators that resonate with stakeholders and align with organizational goals, avoiding information overload.

- **Visualize Data:** Leverage charts, graphs, and visual aids to present data in a visually appealing and easily digestible format, facilitating understanding and retention.

- **Provide Context:** Offer insights and contextualize the data to provide a deeper understanding of the underlying trends, challenges, and opportunities.

- **Tailor Messaging:** Customize the messaging and level of detail according to the preferences and expertise of the stakeholders, ensuring relevance and engagement.

- **Offer Recommendations:** Accompany the report with actionable recommendations for further optimization and improvement, demonstrating a proactive approach to addressing challenges and maximizing opportunities.

By delivering comprehensive and insightful reports, marketers can foster trust, transparency, and collaboration with stakeholders, paving the way for continued support and investment in lead generation initiatives.

10.5 Iterating and Improving Your Lead Generation Strategies

In the ever-evolving landscape of digital marketing, adaptation and iteration are key to staying ahead of the curve. Wishpond facilitates continuous improvement by providing tools for A/B testing, performance tracking, and data analysis to iteratively refine lead generation strategies.

To iterate and improve your lead generation strategies with Wishpond:

- **Perform Regular Audits:** Conduct regular audits of your campaigns to identify areas for improvement and optimization, addressing issues such as audience targeting, messaging effectiveness, and conversion optimization.

- **Experiment with Variations:** Utilize A/B testing to experiment with different elements of your campaigns, such as ad copy, visuals, landing page design, and call-to-action buttons, to identify the most effective combinations.

- **Track Performance:** Monitor campaign performance closely using Wishpond Analytics, paying attention to key metrics such as conversion rates, cost per lead, and ROI, to identify trends and areas for adjustment.

- **Stay Agile:** Remain agile and responsive to changes in market dynamics, consumer behavior, and competitive landscape, adjusting strategies and tactics accordingly to capitalize on emerging opportunities and mitigate risks.

By embracing a culture of experimentation and continuous improvement, businesses can adapt to changing market conditions, optimize lead generation efforts, and drive sustainable growth with Wishpond.

10.6 Celebrating Successes and Setting New Goals

Amidst the rigors of data analysis and performance optimization, it's essential not to overlook the importance of celebrating successes and setting new goals. Wishpond provides a platform for acknowledging achievements, fostering team morale, and charting the course for future growth and innovation.

When celebrating successes and setting new goals with Wishpond:

- **Acknowledge Milestones:** Take the time to recognize and celebrate significant milestones and achievements, whether it's surpassing a lead generation target, achieving a stellar ROI, or winning industry accolades.

- **Reflect on Lessons Learned:** Reflect on lessons learned from past campaigns, identifying key insights, best practices, and areas for improvement to inform future strategies and tactics.

- **Set Stretch Goals:** Challenge your team to set ambitious yet achievable goals that push the boundaries of performance and innovation, fostering a culture of continuous growth and excellence.

- **Collaborate and Inspire:** Foster collaboration and cross-functional alignment by involving team members in the goal-setting process, encouraging diversity of perspectives and collective ownership of objectives.

- **Embrace Innovation:** Encourage experimentation and innovation by exploring new technologies, channels, and strategies to drive lead generation effectiveness and differentiation in the marketplace.

By celebrating successes, reflecting on lessons learned, and setting ambitious goals, businesses can harness the full potential of Wishpond and propel their lead generation efforts to new heights of success and impact.

Conclusion

In concluding our journey through "The Ultimate Wishpond Lead Generation Guide," it's essential to reflect on the transformative power that Wishpond brings to your lead generation efforts. Throughout this guide, we've explored the multifaceted capabilities of Wishpond, from creating compelling landing pages to orchestrating sophisticated email marketing campaigns, harnessing the power of social media, and implementing efficient marketing automation.

By understanding the nuances of Wishpond and implementing its features strategically, you're not merely leveraging a tool; you're unlocking the potential to cultivate meaningful relationships with your audience, drive conversions, and ultimately propel your business forward. Wishpond empowers you to connect with your target market in innovative ways, delivering personalized experiences that resonate and inspire action.

As you embark on your journey with Wishpond, remember that success in lead generation is not just about the tools you use but also about the strategies you employ and the dedication you bring to refining and optimizing your approach. Continuously monitor your campaigns, analyze data insights, and adapt to evolving trends and consumer behaviors.

Moreover, never underestimate the value of experimentation and creativity. Wishpond provides a robust platform for testing ideas, refining your messaging, and uncovering what truly resonates with your audience. Embrace the spirit of innovation, and don't be afraid to think outside the box as you strive to differentiate your brand and capture the attention of your prospects.

Finally, remember that success in lead generation is a journey, not a destination. Celebrate your victories, learn from your setbacks, and always remain committed to the pursuit of excellence. With Wishpond as your partner, the possibilities are endless, and the path to sustainable growth lies within your reach.

Thank you for joining us on this journey. May your endeavors with Wishpond lead you to newfound heights of success and prosperity.

www.ingramcontent.com/pod-product-compliance
Lightning Source LLC
Chambersburg PA
CBHW070156230526